STUBBY

A TRUE STORY OF FRIENDSHIP

First published in Great Britain in 2018 by Andersen Press Ltd.,

20 Vauxhall Bridge Road, London SW1V 2SA.

Copyright © Michael Foreman, 2018.

Photograph of Stubby copyright © Bettmann/ Getty

The right of Michael Foreman to be identified as the

author and illustrator of this work has been asserted by him

in accordance with the Copyright, Designs and Patents Act, 1988.

All rights reserved.

Colour separated in Switzerland by Photolitho AG, Zürich.

Printed and bound in Malaysia.

1   3   5   7   9   8   6   4   2

British Library Cataloguing in Publication Data available.

ISBN 978 1 78344 743 5

STUBBY

A TRUE STORY OF FRIENDSHIP

MICHAEL FOREMAN

Ⓐ

ANDERSEN PRESS

It's hard work being a soldier. Marching, marching every day, getting ready to go to war, but I'm told my country needs me.

This war is far away — the other side of the ocean — but soon we will have to cross that ocean and help to win it.

We are woken up early every morning by a
'toot, toot, toot' on a bugle for yet another day
of marching and shooting practice.

My favourite bugle call is the one that means,
'Grub's up! Come and get it!'

The smell of cooking seems to attract all the stray dogs from miles around. One dog in particular seems to find me every time I settle down to my sausage and mash.

He is an odd little dog with a flat face and short legs. I decide to call him Stubby.

Now Stubby follows me everywhere. The other soldiers
laugh when they see him marching along beside us.
I teach him to 'sit up and beg' for his food and 'sit up and
salute' when he sees an officer. The officers like him too.
Stubby seems one of us now. I know I will miss him
when we go off to war.

Well, that day has arrived. We march to the train station and begin to climb aboard. Stubby has marched with us, of course, and he looks up into my eyes. I can't resist picking him up to hug him goodbye. One of the officers smiles and gives me a wink. I pop Stubby into the carriage with the other men and Stubby gives the officer a salute.

At first, Stubby seems alarmed by the rattle, rattle of the train and the countryside whooshing past the windows, but we share our food with him and he begins to enjoy himself.

The troop ship *Minnesota* is huge and towers over us as we begin to board. I wrap Stubby in a blanket and a group of us smuggle him onto the ship.

When the *Minnesota* is well out to sea, I take
Stubby out onto the deck. The sailors now think
Stubby is the official mascot of our regiment
and I teach him to salute the ship's officers.

Stubby loves standing right at the bow of
the ship to feel the wind through his whiskers.

After many days at sea we see land on the distant horizon.
I feel a mixture of relief and fear. Relief to see dry land at
last, but fear because it is a land at war.

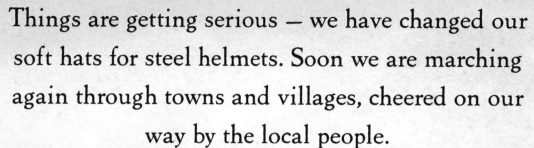

Things are getting serious — we have changed our soft hats for steel helmets. Soon we are marching again through towns and villages, cheered on our way by the local people.

Stubby always gets the loudest cheers, especially from the children, and he is never short of tasty titbits.

After two days of marching, we hear the
thunder of distant guns. The villages
here are deserted and in ruins.

Now we are living in a world of mud, stuck in trenches for weeks. Slowly, slowly moving forward, pushing the enemy back.

Dogs can hear better than humans, so Stubby becomes a very good guard dog, warning us of approaching enemy soldiers. One night, he finds an enemy soldier spying on us, catches him by the seat of his trousers and won't let him go.

Often, Stubby's amazing sense of smell warns us of poison gas attacks. We all put on our gas masks, and Stubby's too. He has become an important member of our company.

At night we try to sleep in muddy trenches. It is cold and Stubby and I snuggle to get warm, but we cannot sleep. All night long the sky is lit up by thunderous gunfire.

At dawn, an officer blows a whistle and we
clamber out of the safety of our trench and charge
towards the enemy guns. I tell Stubby to stay safe

in the trench, but he follows me anyway.
Bullets are zipping and whistling around us. I
see some of our friends fall into the sea of mud.

A deafening BANG and a flash knock me off my feet. The whole world seems to turn over. I see Stubby up in the air flying.

He's off to heaven, I think. Then with a SPLUD
he thuds back down into the thick mud.

I crawl towards him. He is covered
in mud and blood, his eyes full of
pain, looking at me.

"I'm sorry, old friend. I'm sorry I brought you to this stupid war."
I wrap him up in my jacket and carry him back to our trench.

Army doctors take him gently from me and bandage
him up just like the other wounded soldiers. He is
placed carefully into an ambulance with the other
wounded and driven away. Will I ever see him again?

We hear he has been very popular in the hospital, limping around between the beds, saluting all the wounded soldiers.

After six long weeks of terrible fighting we are all cheered up by the return of Stubby.

When we drive the enemy out of a nearby town, some
of the local ladies make Stubby an army jacket, complete
with badges and medals, with his name stitched into it.
He looks so smart that even the officers salute him!

At the eleventh hour, on the eleventh day of the eleventh month, 1918, peace is declared. The war is over!

Soldiers from both sides lay down their guns and climb out of their trenches. Winners or losers, we are all survivors. The enemy are young men like us, and we all just want to go home.

This time, we don't need to hide Stubby
when we climb aboard the troop ship to
cross the ocean. He is a hero.

When we get back home, Stubby is given a position
of honour at the front of the great Victory Parade.
Bands are playing and the streets are crowded with
thousands of people waving flags and cheering.

Peace is wonderful — but peace and quiet
will be even better. I am so thankful this
little stray dog found me.

In 1917, with the First World War already underway, a stray dog wandered into an army training session in Connecticut, USA, looking for scraps of food. The soldiers named him 'Stubby'. Corporal Robert Conroy took to him immediately, and the pair soon became inseparable.

On the front line, Stubby performed many heroic deeds. He would bark warnings to the soldiers of incoming raids or gas attacks, which he could always sense before them. He would patrol for rats and help to find the wounded on the battlefield. After the unit helped to liberate the French town Château-Thierry, the local women made Stubby his very own uniform.

On November 11th, 1918, an armistice was declared and the fighting was over. The entire Yankee Division declared Stubby as their mascot, and when President Woodrow Wilson visited them in France on Christmas Day, 1918, he met Stubby and shook his paw.

After the war, Stubby returned to the USA with Conroy, leading the 102nd Regiment of the Yankee Division in the Boston victory parade on April 25th, 1919.

Stubby enjoyed fame and recognition — he even visited the White House twice, where he met two US presidents: President Harding and President Coolidge.

In 1926, Stubby died peacefully of old age in Conroy's arms, friends forever.